Gymnastics:

Your Best Meet Ever!

Rita Brown

RJC Publishing / Longwood, Florida

Gymnastics: Your Best Meet Ever!
Rita Brown with Rik Feeney
© 2013 by Rita Brown
ISBN: 978-1-938975-00-4 (paperback)
        978-1-938975-01-1 (Kindle)

RJC Publishing
2716 Deer Berry Court
Longwood, FL 32779
info@gymcert.com
www.gymcert.com

DISCLAIMER
This book is written and intended to be used as a guide only. The publisher and author are not engaged in the profession of rendering any form of legal, technical, or medical advice. If for any reason legal, technical or medical advice is necessary, you should seek out qualified professionals.

The purpose of this book is to educate and acquaint individuals with the basics of gymnastics competition. Every effort has been made to provide complete and accurate information on this subject. Readers of this book are strongly advised to seek and obtain professional guidance and instruction from recognized leaders in competitive gymnastics, Gymcert publications, USAG Safety Certified Coaches or Instructors or Coaches with Risk Management Certifications through the USAG (USA Gymnastics).

The author and RJC Publishing shall have neither liability nor responsibility to any person or entity with respect to any injury, loss, or damage caused or alleged to be caused directly or indirectly by the information contained in this book.

Cover Design: Kurt Merkel / Rik Feeney / Rita Brown
Illustrations & Photographs:
Chris Korotky /Lloyd Smith/ Inside Gymnastics
Rita Brown/Jenn Brown
Book Layout & Design:
Rik Feeney / **www.PublishingSuccessOnline.com**

Dedication

This book is dedicated to the Olympic gymnasts that I have had the honor and privilege to work and coach day after day, as Brown's Gymnastics was home to many. My most pride and admiration is summed up by the Olympic results of my following athletes; Brandy Johnson, Wendy Bruce, Eileen Diaz, Carly Patterson and Mohini Bhardwaj. These are the most recognizable female names that reached greatness and fame that trained at Brown's Gymnastics but many others have passed through the doors over the past 32 years and they too are a part of the reason I have so much love and dedication to the wonderful sport of gymnastics!

To my daughter Jenn Brown, who exemplifies life and all it has to offer. Jenn is two-time Emmy Award winning female sportscaster. She works for ESPN covering College Football, College Baseball, XGames and contributes interviews and reports for ESPN *SportsCenter.* Jenn has enthusiastically encouraged me to continue to write and give back to the sport I so love.

Rita Brown with daughter, Jenn Brown at 2012 Olympics

Acknowledgment

The writing of this book has been a long project, and I have to thank Rik Feeney for his patience and encouragement. Your confidence and support are greatly appreciated.

Thanks to Chris Korotky and the "Inside Gymnastics Magazine" for contributing to many of the awesome photographs.

I want to thank USA Gymnastics for assigning me to represent them and the USA in so many international competitions. The feeling of victory when you see your athlete standing on the podium at the Olympics and World Championships award ceremony is awesome and overwhelming.

Rita Brown

**Reprinted by permission of
Inside Gymnastics magazine.**

Table of Contents

Introduction

Bang! You punch through the vault board and fly fully extended toward the vault table. With your body in perfect alignment you punch through your shoulders and block off the vault table soaring through the air to a perfect landing with no steps. The crowd goes wild as you turn and salute the judges, then rush back into the waiting arms of your teammates and coaches who are all smiles and congratulations.

Seconds later the score is flashed... a 9.20! You have finally broken through and scored your first 9.00 on Vault. All the hard work, focus, and attitude during practice really seem worth it now.

And that really is the key to have your best meet ever; preparation, focus, and attitude.

It's not what you do...

As with any activity in life, *"it is not what you do, but how you do it,"* that is important.

As a competitive gymnast, I can remember tumbling across the floor and flicking my head after landing a layout with a full twist to get my hair out of my eyes much to the annoyance of my coach who claimed if I did the hair flick in practice, I would do it in a meet.

Of course, in a meet that is a deduction of a tenth or two, which could mean the difference between being on the medals platform or watching the winners from the stands.

I boldly stated that would never happen.

Seizing the opportunity, my coach bet me I would flick my hair in a meet, and if I did, I would have to get my hair cut to keep it out of my eyes.

With confidence, and a generous helping of arrogance, I accepted the bet.

Practice makes permanent

The moral of the story is, if you practice a bad habit, you will get a bad habit. Even though I told myself not to do it, my body was on autopilot and the next move after landing was always the hair flick, which I performed flawlessly, much to the delight of my coach, who had been trying to get me to cut my hair anyway.

The day after the meet, I sat in a chair in a total state of bewilderment as I watched my mother cut my bangs and some of my luxurious brown hair fell to the floor.

The lesson

Listen to your coach, whether it be strength, flexibility, routine work, or cooperating with other gymnasts during workouts. They may have been gymnasts once and can keep you from making many of the same mistakes they made.

The long and (now) short of it is that no matter what aspect of the competitive goal you are working on the philosophy is the same, **always do your best**.

Every winner was once a beginner

You can't run. You can't hide. You joined the gymnastics team to one day make it into competition. Well, that day may be today.

Are you going to be nervous? Probably.

Will you make some mistakes? Definitely.

Is that a reason to give up? Absolutely not!

You need to accept the fact that you need to make mistakes in order to learn. Competition experience comes from past mistakes that you have corrected so you constantly improve from one meet to the next.

Give yourself permission to fail

The worst thing you can think or say in any gymnastics situation whether it is practice or competition is "I can't!"

Being in competition is like the first time you did a new skill. If you just stood there and said "I can't" your coach had nothing to say that would help you improve.

If you embrace the idea of "I'll do my best!" you will improve much quicker.

Saying "I'll do my best does not confer magical abilities to complete skills perfectly, but it does allow your brain to apply your full resources to the skill.

If you make the skill; fantastic! If you don't make the skill, at least you have applied your best effort and your coach will be able to give you feedback that will help you improve much quicker.

If you maintain the attitude of "I'll do my best" at your first and every competition afterward, your coach has much better information to base his/her coaching decisions on and help you perform even better in the next meet.

Give 100% in practice and at the meet

You really cannot play it safe if you are planning to get the best score possible.

If you don't punch the vault table as hard as you can, how will you learn to control a landing from that much power? You will not magically develop that skill at a championship meet when you "finally" decide to go for it all out.

Magical Techniques

Beyond listening to your coach and always giving your best effort are four magical techniques that separate the gymnast that has success in competition sometimes from the successful competitor.

The keys are:

1. Goal setting

2. Preparation

3. Focus

4. Attitude

Goal Setting & Getting

I want to make the Olympic team!

That may be fine as an ultra-long term goal, but your focus, until you are an elite level athlete, should be on the short term – like just this season.

What are your main goals for just this season?

Let's say your goal is to win the all around title at the state championships this year. If you work backward from the awards platform at state championships, what would the season look like?

- I am the State Champion in the all around competition. (*Yeah!*)

- Focus on going full out on my routines so I can control each of the elements under full power and stick all my landings perfectly.

Rita Brown

- Refine my routines in each of the invitational meets so I am adding a minimum of a full point to my all around score each meet.

- Attend the first invitational meet of the season and make the qualifying score for state championships.

- Successfully perform the whole routine with confidence and competence enough to score a minimum of an 8.00 or better on each event.

- Successfully perform the whole routine without any falls or major wobbles.

- Perform the whole routine.

- Successfully perform the back half of each routine.

- Successfully perform the front half of each routine.

- Be able to perform each of the elements required on each event in a sequence of three or four skills.

- Be able to perform each of the elements required on each event.

- Develop physical strength and flexibility to the highest level you can based on guidelines provided by your coach.

Talk to your coach about the appropriate timeline for each of these steps in your goal ladder to becoming state champion. *(See State Champion Goal Plan in appendix.)*

What's Important Now? (W.I.N.)

You act based on your currently dominant thought (or goals of the moment). A basic goal, like taking care of an annoying itch, is accomplished by the action of scratching.

ACTION is the key word.

The ability to take consistent action towards your goals and desires while responding appropriately to the feedback produced by such actions is the key to your success. You take the action and your coach will give you the feedback.

But, *you* must be willing to take consistent action towards the goal you have established – becoming all around state champion. That does not mean once in a while you go to workout, or, you take a turn every now and then and spend the rest of the time chatting around the chalk box.

It means that every single day and every single moment of workout you do something that moves you toward your goal, no matter how small that action may be. It also means that you will do whatever it takes to reach that goal, staying within the bounds of appropriate workout behavior and basic rules of courtesy.

Note: Workouts are nothing like what you may have seen on TV shows.

Everything is connected

Every goal you have will interact in some way with every other goal you have. Pretend that all the facets of your life (home, school, friends, and hobbies) are all part of a mobile, like the one that used to hang over your crib when you were an infant. If you tug on any one part of the mobile, you affect every other part, sending all the parts into motion.

Every goal you have, no matter how big or small, will affect every other goal you have including your goal to be a state champion. Keep this in mind when making your plans.

Goal setting is a lifelong skill and clearly defined goals are the key to staying focused on the tasks necessary for a successful competitive season.

Each goal should be clearly defined and within your grasp with appropriately applied effort.

How To Achieve All Your Goals

The basics for achieving any goal you have are:

1) Define exactly what your goal is. To some extent we have already done that with the goal ladder above. Of course, if your goal is different, make changes in the goal ladder appropriate to your needs. Just be specific.

Saying, "I want to score better on my bar routine." is too vague. Be more specific, like, "I will cast to the required height or higher out of my glide kip to get a better score on bars."

2) Take Action to achieve your goal. Do something, anything that will begin to make this goal a reality. Beginning is the hardest part in achieving a goal. Most of us tend to put things off until a later date. Do something to achieve your goal now.

The very first thing you can do to take action toward your goal is **Ask Questions.**

ASK stands for Always Seek Knowledge.

If your goal is to cast higher on bars, ask your coach what improvements you could make to your kip, or what strength exercises you can do to improve your cast.

Your coach will likely always be the first person to ask about any gymnastics goal you have.

3) Act "As If." Act as if you have already achieved your goal. Visualize in words, pictures, and emotions exactly what it feels like to achieve your goal and then behave "as if" the goal is already an accomplishment in your life.

4) Accept Feedback from your coach and use this information to adjust your strategy to achieve your goal. To succeed in any endeavor you must have experience. To get experience you must be willing to make mistakes. Each mistake is feedback on your road to the successful accomplishment of your goal.

If your goal is to see a sunrise, and you are facing west, you may need to change your strategy. Study the feedback from each attempt toward your goal and determine whether it is in your best interests to continue with the same strategy or adapt and change it to reach your goal.

5) Do Whatever It Takes! You must do whatever it takes to achieve your goal. If it means you have to wake an hour earlier each day for study or to complete obligations at home - do it!

These are the basics of how to achieve your goal of becoming a state champion in the all around, or for practically any other goal you may have.

Review your goals

Every now and then go back and review each goal. Once it has been accomplished give yourself a smiley face, a gold star, or at the minimum, pat yourself on the back and say, "Well done me!"

Note: Also see "Specific Meet Goals" list in the appendix.

Life changes to keep in mind

- At the lower team levels the number of hours of practice per week is relatively few. As you progress up the competitive ladder the hours and days of workout will continue to build and cut into your social, school, and family time.

- Your parents will have to change their schedules and possibly eliminate some of their activities to be available to drive you to practice and pick you up. Talk to your teammates and see if you can carpool.

- Gymnastics competitions will take up a number of weekends during the competitive season.

- Homework will have to be done much more efficiently and with better study habits due to shorter periods of time available. (See "Homework Guidelines" in the appendix.)

- Time management skills will become a necessity in all areas of your life *(and your parents).* You will have less time at home and less time to spend with friends outside the sphere of gymnastics influence.

- On the bright side you will be hanging out with other athletes who are committed to excellence and doing skills most of the rest of the world consider impossible.

- You get to wear super cool leotards that make you look like a super hero. In fact, after your gymnastics career you may become a super hero on the silver screen or at least perform the stunts for the super hero.

Rita Brown

Reprinted by permission of Inside Gymnastics magazine.

Preparation

Conditioning

If ever there was a magical technique that could guarantee your best performance at a gymnastics competition, it would be conditioning.

I sincerely believe that the difference between the few who consistently perform well at competitions and those that have only fleeting success is their level of conditioning.

When you are strong enough to literally grip the beam with your toes and hold yourself on after a slight wobble or power through the finish of a long hang kip, you know you have a level of control that most of the other competitors can only dream about.

In addition, it is possible that a certain amount of fear is the body's unconscious acknowledgment that you may not be strong enough to fully control the skill.

Strength evaluation

Talk to your coach and let him/her know what skills you still have concerns, that is you may not be making them consistently or they are a cause of concern (just a little bit of fear).

Once the above skills have been identified, your coach can prescribe a series of strength drills and exercises to solve the problem.

Gymnasts that put 100% into their strength training are usually the ones accepting medals on the awards platform at competitions.

Strength training cycles

Your strength training may vary depending on the time of year. Usually during the summer and the fall you will spend more time doing traditional exercises like push-ups, sit-ups, and leg lifts. As you get closer to the season, your coach will likely adjust your strength training until you are doing what is known as sport or skill specific exercises. In other words, to build up your strength for glide kips you coach may have you do sets of three glide kips. On floor, you may do several passes of round off to two or three back handsprings.

Conditioning – Flexibility

Another important aspect of conditioning is flexibility or the range of motion a body part can pass through safely while maintaining control.

Yup, that means taking the time to completely stretch out after every workout. Every excuse in the world has been made to leave workout early, all seemingly plausible, but the bottom line is that a lack of flexibility can affect the performance of your skills and open you to the possibility of injury. So, stay and stretch at the end of every workout.

Competition advantage

You may be wondering what this has to do with excellence in competition. Those gymnasts' in peak condition can cast higher on bars, punch harder on vault, and when things go slightly sideways they can perform what many call the miracle save.

So, with regard to preparation, conditioning is definitely one of the magical techniques in producing success.

Technical Preparation

"Vertical height is equal to the square of the horizontal velocity if the takeoff angle is before 90-degrees..."

What?

Exactly, if you don't understand something your coach is teaching, ask him/her to repeat it in even simpler terms.

ASK = Always Seek Knowledge

The key is to ask questions or Always Seek Knowledge until you are so sure of what your coach is asking you to do that you can feed the information back to him/her in your own words.

Once you know what to do, when to do it, and how to perform it safely, you can perform the skill with confidence and certainly with a greater degree of safety.

Preparation – Calendar of Events

Planning all aspects of your season in advance is a great way to relieve stress that seems to have no known cause.

Seasonal Calendar

One good idea is to go to some office supply store and buy an 8.5 X 11 inch monthly calendar and plan out your year.

First, mark off all the major holidays and potential trips you may take during those dates, like visiting grandma for Thanksgiving or the holidays.

Next, mark off all school breaks, then go back and mark off and special school functions like dances, football ames, final exams, SAT's or other exceptional events.

Note: Just because I ask you to mark off events like football games or dances, that does not mean you automatically get to attend those events. That is something that you need to work out with your coach, especially if there will be a competition on the same weekend.

Finally, mark off all the gymnastics competitions you will attend that year and any associated travel dates.

Where does the time go?

Once you have filled out your calendar, you will have a visual reference of what your year will look like. If you are like many young gymnasts, your schedule is probably quite busy.

Using your calendar you can make sure scheduling conflicts do not occur, or if they do, you can plan way in advance to make those times easier to deal with.

For instance, if you know a qualifying meet may be around the time you are taking a big test in school, you can plan to work around it by doing some extra studying ahead of time and working with your teacher to develop study plans.

Gymnastics: Your Best Meet Ever!

**Reprinted by permission of
Inside Gymnastics magazine.**

Preparing for Competition:

Eliminating Worry

Without a plan of action, you may find yourself worrying about minor details.

Worrying is the inability to make a decision regarding a specific situation.

Do you really need that kind of stress when you are trying to focus on a successful competition?

Making a conscious choice for any situation (worry) will relax your mind and allow you to concentrate on what is important – the successful performance of your gymnastics routines.

Following are action plans for the most common situations every gymnast faces prior to competition.

Travel and timing

Since you probably don't drive yet, you need to make sure your parents get all the information about the meet location, when open warm-ups start, and about how long the meet is.

- Post the dates of your competitions in a prominent place, like the front of your refrigerator. Better yet, make sure the dates are listed on your parent's planners or computer schedule programs.

- Google or MapQuest the directions to the meet, but since these directions can sometimes be confusing, get a copy of a real map to bring with you.

- You might also want to get your coach's cell phone number in case you get lost so you can give him/her a heads up or get directions.

- If you are staying over the night before you might want to do a practice run driving over to the site of the meet with your parents to check parking and potential construction delays.

Please keep in mind that most competitions are not held at the address of the gymnastic club that is sponsoring the event, although you may be able to get maps and other pertinent meet information from the club's website.

What to bring

The night before the meet, put everything you need in your gym bag. Ask your coach to review a list of necessities, or you can check the "Gym Bag Necessities" list in appendix of this book.

Waking up

You know how long it normally takes to "get it all together" in the morning. You need to wake up in plenty of time to be alert and focused for the competition, so make sure you get plenty of sleep the night before.

In addition, you want to eat early enough that your food is digested.

Put some fruits, veggies, crackers, and some water in your gym bag in case there is a delay in competition and you develop some hunger pangs.

Equipment settings

Make sure you know your settings for uneven bars, vault, and beam. Bring a little notepad or piece of paper and pen to record your settings.

Warm up strategy

Stay focused and take advantage of your warm-up turns, since there may be several other gymnasts waiting in line.

If you miss a skill, don't jump off and pout. Quickly remount and finish your turn.

Remember, warm-ups don't necessarily predict what will happen in the meet, so don't get "psyched out" beforehand.

If you spend most of your warm-up watching others perform, that means you aren't thinking about your own routines.

Forget about everyone else.

Talk to your coach to develop a warm up strategy. What skills or sequences should you focus on most? Doing skills that you have rock solid may not be the best use of your warm up time. Focus on the most important skills and sequences.

Competition

Follow the rules of the competition and stay with your rotation.

Avoid looking or talking to your parents or other spectators. Absolutely no texting during competition!

Concentrate on your coach's instructions.

Keep your competition gear safely inside your gym bag throughout the meet, unless you are currently using it. Keep your gym bag under your chair or in a place where it will not hinder traffic or cause a problem near the competition apparatus.

Judges

Before and after each routine you are required to present yourself to the judges by saluting.

When doing so, look the head judge directly in the eyes with a calm, confident expression.

Regardless of what happens during the routine, never show your displeasure to the judges (or the audience) afterward.

Even if you missed one of your skills, the judges may not have noticed if you covered well, but they will notice a bad attitude.

The best thing you can wear to a competition is a great big smile which you give away freely.

Scores

A score is not a judgment of you as an individual.

A score is an evaluation of a single performance.

Once you have completed a routine, leave it behind and concentrate on the next event.

Falls

If you should fall or have a major break in a routine, take the time to mentally prepare for the rest of the exercise.

Check to see if you injured yourself.

Chalk up again, if necessary. Once you are mentally composed, continue your routine as though you never had the break.

It may be better to take a few extra moments to get focused, regardless of a minor deduction from your score. Consult with your coach.

Enjoy the moment

Learn how to enjoy yourself at meets.

Lessons are learned in both success and failure. Remember the formula Event + Response = Outcome.

It's easy to enjoy the outcome when successful; the mark of a champion is learning to enjoy the process regardless of the outcome.

Have fun at your next competition.

Reprinted by permission of
Inside Gymnastics magazine.

Nutrition

Nutrition cannot be dictated

Obviously, you eat what your parents prepare daily and you are capable of performing appropriately in workouts.

The suggestions listed here are designed to optimize performance the day of the meet.

Special nutritional guidelines for elite performers are designed by a certified nutritionist, if necessary.

Breakfast of Champions?

Nutrition is a topic for debate in sports and life in general. Does anybody really have a foolproof system of eating?

If you go in to any book store you will see literally hundreds of diet books that all claim to be the ultimate in information on proper nutrition.

If you watch morning talk shows you will notice several media darling doctors also claiming to have the latest information on nutrition and likely also have a special supplement or proprietary diet program to sell you.

Even the U.S. government has recently changed the "food pyramid". What does that say for all the nutritional information put out that used the original food pyramid as a guideline?

What is a diet anyway?

Your diet is what you currently eat. All these media based diets are actually "restricted diets" where for a certain time you eat specified foods, cut calories, or add exercise.

In my mind, there really are only three ways to lose weight, and they are: 1) cut back the calories, 2) add physical activities to burn more calories, or 3) combine 1 & 2 by adding more activity and cutting out the empty calories.

My favorite of the methods is #3, adding activity and cutting out empty calories.

Empty calories are things like soda, gum, candy, and excess snack foods.

Access your inner cavewoman

The human body's needs for food are not all that different from your cavewoman ancestor's several thousand years ago. The problem is technology has increasingly changed natural foods into look-alikes that are stuffed with fillers, additives, and chemicals designed to prolong the shelf life of each product.

In my opinion, none of that can be too good for the human body.

Eat what grows

Quite likely, the best thing you can do for your health and provide you with the optimum nutrition for great competitions is to eat what grows naturally, whether that is animal or vegetable.

What about fast food?

If you treat fast food like dessert, that is, you only eat it once in a while as a treat you will be fine. You may actually find that eating naturally grown foods may soon make fast food less palatable.

You need to lose weight!

Who said so?

Be very careful who you listen to with regard to weight loss issues.

Weight is irrelevant

First, you should know that your weight is actually irrelevant. It is the ratio of fat versus lean muscle tissue and bone that is important.

The most effective way to find that ratio is with underwater weighing by a sports medical doctor with nutrition training.

Once you know what percentage of your bodyweight is fat and a doctor has determined for your height, build, and bone structure what weight is optimal for you, then you can determine a plan to increase activity and cut back calories effectively to reach your goal weight.

A plan for all athletes

It might be a good idea to find out what your basal metabolic rate is – that is how many calories you need to burn a day to maintain your current body weight.

Knowing your specific caloric needs will help you make better food choices each day.

Track your calories

Another bit of information you will need is a tracking chart of everything you eat for at least two to three weeks – and I mean everything you eat.

On the internet or in one of the many book stores you can find calorie guides that will let you know what the calorie count is for the amount of food eaten. Accurately track the food and the quantity (number of ounces) for every single thing that goes in your mouth for two to three weeks – a month is even better.

Track your weight

In addition, every morning (at the same time) for the month that you track your food intake, record your weight for that day. Please remember, that your weight at this point is not an important factor.

Muscle is heavier than fat

One of the reasons that weight, by itself, is not important as an evaluation of your level of fitness is that muscle can weigh up to three times more than fat.

Two athletes standing side by side could weigh the exact same amount, but one athlete may be much leaner and have more muscle, so will weigh the same as the other athlete but be in much better shape.

Splurging

Once in a while having a hot fudge sundae is great! Eating a sundae for breakfast, lunch, and dinner is definitely not the best idea. The same goes for any type of food.

The key is to eat all foods in moderation.

Depriving yourself of foods you love is only going to make you crave them more. You can eat almost anything you want; you just need to regulate the quantities appropriate to your goal of having a highly functioning athletic body.

Tightening and toning for competition

Keeping in mind, everything said above, as you progress through the season focusing your training on peaking for championship meets, you may also want to refine your diet so you are eating only the very best foods to help maintain a lean body.

Again, you will want to speak with a doctor of sports medicine with a nutrition background to refine your diet. The key is to create a body for optimum performance, enjoy your meals, and not feel hungry!

Good eating habits

The purpose of this section is to start you on the road to good nutrition for athletic competition and life in general.

Jump into the deep end?

Developing any nutritional program or refined diet should be a gradual, step by step program. Don't go crazy changing everything you eat within a week, take it one step at a time.

Gradually cut back on your soda consumption until you are drinking more water and juice.

Hydration

One of the most essential keys to good nutrition is hydration, in other words drinking water.

Sometimes a thirst for water is mistaken for hunger pangs. Why not find out if you are really just thirsty first by drinking a large glass of water. If 15-20 minutes later you still feel hungry then you can get something to eat.

If you live in a particularly hot or humid climate you may need to get a drink more often to keep from becoming dehydrated.

Eating before the meet

Previous to a competition, the idea is to eat foods that are easily digested and will supply you with energy.

Breakfast foods like oatmeal, whole grain or high-fiber cereal, muffins, and all types of fruit are good choices.

Lunches and dinners can come from the salad bar where there are a wide variety of choices.

The idea is not to bog your digestive system with excess meats, fried or fatty food, or any food that causes you distress.

In general, you should finish your meal at least an hour before warm ups begin. Otherwise, the food lies like a lump in your stomach while the body diverts blood flow to your arm and leg muscles, which are now demanding priority as you become more active.

Carry a small snack (health bars, crackers, fruits) and a fruit juice drink and/or water in your gym bag to stave off hunger pangs should they arise during a competition.

Summary

If you focus on eating foods that are naturally grown and not cooked in deep fats you are on your way to a more beneficial way of eating, especially for an athlete.

Also keep in mind that you can eat pretty much anything as long as you eat in moderation.

And finally, drink lots of water. In fact, you may want to make it your beverage of choice. Water will help wash out toxins in the body and make you feel much better than if you are drinking several empty calories via sodas and high sugared/processed juices.

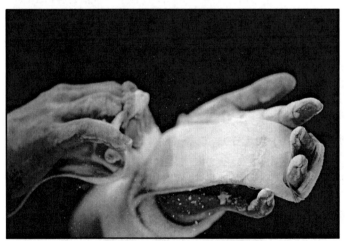

**Reprinted by permission of
Inside Gymnastics magazine.**

The purpose of this meet...

Meets have different meanings and the training for each will differ accordingly.

Some meets, the focus may only be on obtaining a **qualifying score** for the state championship meet, therefore a coach may tone down the power and have you focus on higher quality execution.

Mobility meets are set up for a gymnast to obtain a specific score so she can move to the next competitive level. The coach may not be focusing on you achieving awards in such a meet, instead focusing on obtaining a score that will allow you to move up to the next level of competition.

Another meet might be used to **develop confidence** and the coach may allow you to attempt new skills and/or have you go all out while removing the worry of needing specific scores since in previous meets you have already qualified for championships.

Finally, there is the meet that everyone hopes the coach and gymnast will pull out all the stops – state **championships**, where everyone hopes their efforts from the past year of training and experience in the lead up meets will make them a winner at championships.

Training to peak performance

In some cases the goal for a competition may not be to win at all. Many coaches train their gymnasts to peak for certain meets. "Peaking" is when a gymnast is performing at her highest levels physically and mentally. This phenomenon cannot be sustained for long periods of time, so it must be planned to coincide with the championship level meets in a season.

If you go into a meet at the beginning of the season and attempt to win each event and the all around competition, you may be a winner for the day, however, you may also end up peaking too soon and end up somewhere in the middle of the pack by the time the championship meets are held.

A coach can set the pace for how soon you "peak" in your competitive performance by planning the workouts so you build your routines throughout the beginning part of the season and perfect them as the meets progress and you qualify to championship meets.

Arousal Control

In addition, the level of arousal (being up and ready for the meet) can play a part in how well you compete. If you get too keyed up, you may blow the performance.

Sometimes a coach needs to calm you down rather than build you up for the competition.

What is the coach's job?

Ideally, at the meet your coach will keep track of when each gymnast competes, the equipment settings for each gymnast, and most important of all the coach will be in charge of arousal control.

Arousal control

Your coach has already spent the whole preseason building up your strength and flexibility, teaching you the skills for your routines, and preparing you for competition by having you do at practice through hundreds of repetitions of the skills and routines exactly what you will now do on autopilot at the meet.

The only job the coach should have at the meet now is controlling your level of motivation (or arousal).

Some gymnasts arrive at the meet ready to jump out of their skins they are so excited. Other gymnasts get to the meet and seem like they are about to fall back asleep.

What kind of gymnast are you? Do you get super excited or are you relatively calm?

What works best for you?

Your coach's job at the meet is to find out what level of motivation works best for you. The coach may need to pump you up at some meets and other meets may need to calm you down. That is what arousal control is all about.

What works at one meet may not work at another, and the coach makes the determination of how much pumping up or calming down you need based on your performance during open and timed warm ups.

Synchronizing your goals
Keep in mind that each meet has a different purpose during the season and you need to ask your coach about the purpose of a particular meet so your goals are in agreement.

Your coach's goal is to make appropriate changes to your routines at each meet for your best possible performance and us e the feedback from the competition to make a plan so you peak (achieve your best performance state) appropriately at the championship meet.

The young gymnast finished her turn and then struck a pose on the balance beam. Squaring her shoulders and taking a deep breath she raised her arms up next to her ears to prepare for her back handspring, and...

Power over FEAR

Frustration and fear often set in when you begin to wonder whether you will be ready or not for competition.

Worrying, the inability to make a decision will only make things worse. Worrying takes away the laser-like focus needed in your workouts to perfect your skills and in some cases may hold you back from even making an attempt at a skill you want to perform in competition and may eventually lead to an unnamable fear you can't seem to shake.

The question is: Are you dealing with true fear or simply the inability to make a decision (worry)?

FEAR

The word fear is made up of four letters (F-E-A-R) which most often stand for False Expectations Appearing Real.

Any gymnast worrying about her preparation will talk to herself in a manner that builds fear by saying things like *"if I don't have this skill ready, then I won't be able to do my whole routine, then I won't be able to be in the meet, my mom will get really mad because she spent all this money and that could cause her blood pressure to rise, and..."*

The example may be a little farfetched, but you would be surprised to hear some of the fears many gymnast's have that are not based on fact, only their own dark imaginings.

Take action

Taking action towards your goal will take your mind off of your problems and focus it towards solutions, which will eliminate worry and help to banish fear.

Gymnastics: Your Best Meet Ever!

Sit down with your coach and determine the specific steps necessary to reach your goals.

In my experience, worry, doubt, and fear usually stem from:

1. A lack of strength or flexibility appropriate to completing the specific skill. Solution: Evaluate the strength and flexibility requirements of the skill and have your coach develop a conditioning program suitable to remedy the problem.

2. A lack of understanding of the technical aspects of the skill. In other words you do not completely understand what it is you are supposed to do. Solution: Ask your coach to break the skill down into smaller parts and provide you with simpler explanations until you can feed back exactly what it is you are supposed to do to the coach.

3. You are not mentally prepared and/or motivated to do the skill. If you are physically prepared and know what to do and still you do not attempt the skill, at some level you simply may not want to do the skill. You choose your behavior and by

extension choose the consequences of that behavior. Perhaps it is a sense of security, or possibly the feeling that you are already at a limit you are comfortable with regarding your routine. Solution: Determine your motivation. Do you really want this skill? If you cannot think of an answer to this dilemma, you may want to contact a sports psychologist to help you uncover the underlying concerns.

Taming your fear

Unfortunately, dealing with the psychology of fear is not always as easy as putting on a different hat, and like the Scarecrow from Oz immediately being endowed with the information necessary to solve the problem.

Coach, psychologist,...

Although the common belief is that sports coaches have significant amounts of training in this area, let me be the first to tell you, I am not a psychologist but I do have a few commonsense ideas you can apply when you experience unusual fear performing a specific skill.

First, beating yourself up mentally is rarely an effective solution to the problem.

You cannot process the reverse of an idea like, "don't do this…" "why can't you do that…" "Stop bending your knees." Talking to yourself in this manner is not productive.

Think about the mental picture that the sentence "Stop bending your knees!" conjures in your mind. You literally see yourself bending your knees.

The key is to focus your verbal and mental cues on what you want, not what you don't want to have happen. In this case, the proper verbal/mental cue would be "This time I will keep my legs straight." Simple. Straightforward. Easy to do.

Comfort zone

Keep in mind that everyone has "comfort zones." Like a thermostat keeps the room temperature constant, your belief system will act like a thermostat to bring you back in line with your beliefs if you get too far out of range.

External motivation from your coach may get you to perform outside your comfort zone temporarily, but your belief system will adjust your skill level back to where you think it belongs before too long.

Beliefs are like stairs in a house. To get to the top usually requires you to ascend one step at a time. Taking the steps two at-a-time or running up too quickly may cause you to falter and literally tumble down the stairs. At this point fear, if not injury, may re-adjust your comfort zone to a lower setting.

The key is success

You may need time to adjust your beliefs to successively higher and higher levels and nothing succeeds like success. Ask your coach to back you up a few steps in technique to a point where you felt both confident and competent, then work yourself back up to the final skill one step at a time as your comfort level increases.

Again, pay attention to your thoughts during this process. Comments like "I can't" often don't really mean you are incapable; more likely you still have some conscious or unconscious concerns. In this case, you want to train yourself to use appropriate verbalizations like, "I'll do my best!"

I'll do my best!

"I'll do my best!" still leaves the possibility for error, but is infinitely more valuable for your coach if each of your attempts is truly your best, because now your coach can be laser-accurate with suggestions for you to improve.

No athlete performs perfectly on each attempt. Take your time and make several attempts at the skill before making any decisions about your improvement.

After several attempts your coach can identify patterns of skill performance and make more accurate technical changes than if you expect a coaching cue after each attempt.

Minimize the fear

Another possibility to help you eliminate fear as an obstacle to skill achievement is to de-magnify any incident specifically associated with the fear.

Wipeouts happen, but they are usually the exception rather than the rule.

Would you give up eating pizza for life if one time you accidentally burned the roof of your mouth with hot cheese?

Would you crawl through life because once you fell down and scraped your knee?

The point is to keep the fear in perspective. You can do this by using the techniques listed in the "Mental Movies" section of this book like imagining the fearful scene trapped inside a balloon that floats up and eventually out of sight.

If the mental picture persists, simply throw a mental brick at the picture and imagine it shattering to be replaced by an appropriate image of you successfully completing the skill.

You, a movie star?

You can also make video or DVD recordings of you successfully performing the skills, which you can watch on your computer, IPOD, or DVD player to reinforce your belief in successfully performing the skill.

Self-talk scripts

You can also develop self-talk scripts to bolster your belief in the successful accomplishment of the skill. Using a USB microphone and software that comes with most computers running some version of Windows™, you can read your script onto an mp3 or .wav file and download them to your iPod. Using the continuous loop function, you can listen to these success scripts in your own voice at night while you sleep.

The consistent layering of success-oriented self-talk scripts intertwined with your mental movies can become steel cables of belief directing your actions and attitudes to confident and successful performance of any gymnastics skill or routine.

Dwelling on the rewards of success rather than the penalties of failure is the key to success and the key to overcoming any fear.

Rita Brown

**Reprinted by permission of
Inside Gymnastics magazine.**

Focus

1. *Follow One Course Until Successful*

2. *Follow One Coach Until Successful*

What helps you focus?

I know some gymnasts that get so in to the competition, watching other routines, cheer leading other teammates, and generally soaking in the whole experience that no other outside stimuli is necessary.

Yet other gymnasts take advantage of technology and put together complete sound tracks for the meet on their iPods or iPhones. They might have musical selections that include the theme from Rocky III, Superman, and other motivational film themes. Other gymnasts put together soundtracks of their favorite music; anything that pumps them up and makes them feel good.

Success movies

Another great thing you can do with you iPod is to cobble together videos of your best routines. Add your favorite music and you have a mini-movie of your successful competition.

If you don't have an iPod, you can always upload your movies to YouTube and access them via your cell phone.

Note: Cell phones are fine for accessing your success movies, but are definitely not okay for texting or even chatting with your parents in the stands or communicating with your friends during a meet.

During the meet you need to stay focused on your goal; competing to the best of your ability and toward that end the word focus stands for *Follow One Coach Until Successful.*

The only coach to pay attention to in competition is the one that trains you every day in the gym and actually has a USAG Professional certification along with Safety Basics certification. Family and

friends have the best of intentions but
they do not have even the remotest idea
of what is best for you during competition.

Attitude

If you can't say anything nice to yourself...

How important are the words you use in your mental dialogue or self-talk during a workout in the gym?

Are you truly coaching yourself toward the goals you want or directing activities through your self-talk toward the inevitable failure in which you believe?

"Can't you get it right?"

"Why aren't you paying attention?"

"You messed it up this time."

This not your coach yelling at you. These are the thoughts and ideas coming from your own mind!

Your self-talk is critical to success and safety.

Can you imagine getting up on a Balance Beam at a meet and saying to yourself, "I hope I stay on, but I'll probably fall and straddle the beam on my next skill."

Ouch! That kind of self-talk is not only detrimental to confidence, it can cause painful consequences.

Comments like, "I can't", or the infamous, "I'll try, but..." (and then add an excuse for failure in advance) are quite common in many gyms.

The range of excuses and negative comments are varied but they have one thing in common; these thoughts are negative associations about some aspect of the gymnast or her capabilities, which, in many cases, have no basis in reality.

Could you be doing the same in your experience of the world?

You need to concentrate your mental language on what you want, not what you don't want to have happen.

For instance, when you attempt a skill and have poor form thinking, "My legs are bent." All you mentally reinforce is "bent legs" and that is what you will be thinking the next time you make an attempt at the skill.

Self talk combined with mental picturing is a powerful force directing your body and actions.

And, your mind does not associate positive or negative attributes to any of your mental pictures.

DON'T SLAM THE CAR DOOR!

No matter what is written here make sure you do not allow the mental image of a car door slamming to come into your mind.

I'll bet you did.

In the same way I caused you to think of a car door slamming, you could unintentionally be concentrating on the reverse of what you want during the performance of a skill.

Self-talk should focus on what you want to achieve to produce better results.

Instead of saying to yourself, "Don't bend your legs," which creates a mental picture in your mind of bent legs, the more appropriate mental cue would be, "Next time, keep your legs straight." Now you have a mental picture of what you need to improve.

The key is to always state in clear terms exactly what you want, not what you don't want mentally, verbally, and physically.

You can communicate negative or positive with facial expressions and body language as easily as you can with words.

In keeping with this theme there are certain questions you never ask a coach, such as: 'What am I doing wrong?"

The correct form of the question is "What can I do better next time?" Always ask positively oriented questions.

Eliminate all negative words and phrases from your vocabulary. Avoid statements like, "I can't," "That's too hard," or any variation on that theme.

One statement you must change is, "I'll try," followed by the inevitable, "but...," and then an excuse in advance for why you might fail.

It is much better to say, "I'll do my best," and then accept whatever coaching advice you get for improvement on the next attempt.

Whether the skill is completed perfectly on each attempt is not important, only that you gave your best effort.

Keys to appropriate self-talk

1. Always state mentally and verbally what you want (to have, do, or be).

2. Adopt the posture and physicality of a person who is confident in achieving her goals.

3. Do your best on each attempt at your goals. Use the experience gained from each attempt to continually learn and adapt your skills.

   (**Note**: If you achieve every goal on the first attempt; your goals are too easy. The fun in life comes from stretching yourself and your abilities and overcoming mistakes and learning from past failures.)

4. Change negatively oriented statements as soon as they occur. This will take continuous practice. We are all proficient in thinking of anything and everything that can go wrong. Be kind to yourself. You have had a lifetime of practicing negative self-talk, it will take at least a "few days" to substitute the old habit with the practice of goal/need/desire -oriented self-talk.

Thought is the ancestor to every action our body makes.

Your mind will work to achieve your currently dominant thought regardless of what it is; so think only about what you want.

Remember, you don't always get what you want on each attempt, but in the long run, you usually get what you expect.

Expect the best.

Movies of the Mind

The mind cannot tell the difference between something that is vividly imagined and that which is real.

Visualization, the ability to picture in your mind a goal, a desire, even a favorite memory has been a successful technique used by athletes for decades to help improve performance and achieve extraordinary goals.

Using your mind to create mental movies of your goals is not a snap your fingers type of solution. Just like you need to physically practice your gymnastics skills, you will need to consistently practice creating mental movies of the successful outcomes of your goals.

Creating mental movies is specific to the individual

Most of the time when I was tumbling, I never "saw" anything during the skill. I only had a physical sense of where I was in the air. That can also be true of mental picturing or making movies in your mind.

Some people picture and see beautiful full color pictures complete with all five senses of sight, sound, feel, taste, and smell.

Other people see pictures in their head in black and white while others get only fleeting or fuzzy glimpses and still others never really see anything at all but get a sense or feeling of thought being pictured.

Don't worry about how you picture right now. When I first started mental picturing to practice my routines, I did not see in my head as much as I felt the routines. After years of practice, however, I can now see readily the mental pictures I desire.

What's in your bedroom?

As soon as I asked that question did a picture of your bed, your dresser, or your closet pop into your head? What about your closet? Is it filled with clothes? Do you have some gymnastics medals arranged on top of your dresser along with a couple of trophies? Do you have stuffed animals on your bed? Is your room messy or neat? How many windows are in your room? What color are the walls painted?

As you accessed each of these memories, did you get at least a fleeting glimpse of that part of your room? If you did, you were mentally picturing your room.

Creating mental movies

Following are the basic steps in practicing your gymnastics skills, routines, and visualizing successful gymnastics competitions.

1) Sit in a comfortable chair with your feet flat on the floor, your hands on the arm of the chair or resting comfortably in your lap.

2) Take in a deep breath through your nose until your chest and stomach are fully expanded and hold for about five seconds, then slowly breathe out through your mouth until your chest and stomach are fully deflated.

Note: Just taking deep breaths in this fashion during a meet, especially just before you compete can help you relax and focus on your best performance.

3) Starting with your toes and feet, then your calves, then your thighs, squeeze each muscle group tight for about five seconds, then relax. Do this with all the muscles in your body.

4) Do the breathing exercise listed in number (2) five more times. By now, you should be fully relaxed. You may also want to imagine being bathed in a radiant gold and white light that spreads down through the top of your head filling your whole body with your concept of good.

5) Now, depending on the goal of your mental movie making, you can start picturing the perfect workout or the most successful competition. *(See the "Competition Script" for an idea of what will occur at a gymnastics competition.)*

6) When you first start creating mental movies you may find your mind will wander and think about other things. This is normal. Simply acknowledge the thought and then return to mental movie making for your gymnastics success.

7) Another common element of mental movie making is negative images. The exact thing you don't want keeps popping into your head.

The only way to remove a negative image is to replace it with something else, something positive.

For instance, say you are doing a back handspring on the balance beam and you see yourself losing your balance and falling off. Immediately freeze the mental picture and rewind it just like you might do with a TiVo or a DVR. Then mentally press play again until you are successfully sticking the back handspring rock solid on the beam with confidence and poise.

Additional ways to replace negative images:

- Freeze the negative action into a stained glass picture and mentally throw a rock through it to reveal the positive action you desire.
- Take the negative picture and shrink it until it is so small you can no longer see it, only the picture of you doing the skill successfully.

- Take the negative picture and literally move it behind you until you can no longer see it and the only thing left is a picture of your success.
- Encase the negative image in a bright blue helium balloon and watch it float away until you can no longer see it.

The ways to rid yourself of negative images are as limitless as your imagination, but remember, you must always replace that image with an image of what you do want.

Improve the quality of your mental movies

The more realistic you make your mental movie the more believable it will be, and you will act accordingly with confidence and confidence.

Five-sense your mental movie

As you play the movie in your mind imagine what the beam feels like beneath your feet, or the jolt you will get when you punch off the vault table. What does the gym smell like? Can you hear the music playing on floor? Have you made yourself accustomed to the sudden cheering for another athlete at some other event? Can you taste the chalk dust in the air? What does the gym smell like?

When you can add all this sensory detail to the movies in your head, they will become more and more vividly alive and effective.

Perspective

A question that some debate is from what point of view you should create your mental movies.

You may see your mental picture from inside your head, or only what you would see as you perform your routine, or you could picture your routine as though you were outside your body and videotaping yourself.

The answer I believe is to picture both ways, but certainly picture what you would see and feel when you are performing the routines.

Note: You may want to ask your parents to videotape your routines at a meet or in practice and splice together the best performances to create a video of your routines being done to the best of your ability. It helps when you can see yourself perform the skills correctly.

Pop quiz!

Stop right now and think of one of your goals. Take a moment to picture it in your mind.

What did you have - a movie, a snapshot, or a feeling?

If it was a picture was it in black and white, or color? Was it dark or brightly lit?

Did the picture seem to be near or far away? Was it in a frame or did it seem to go on forever?

Were there any smells associated with it?

Could you hear anything?

Was it loud or quiet?

Did you taste anything?

Did you "see" anything at all, or did you simply get a feeling associated with your goal? Was the feeling strong or mild? Did you get a feeling of heaviness or lightness?

All of the above is meant to illustrate some of the ways we visualize our goals.

Goals that are strong tend to be brightly lit and seem to be very close at hand for those who picture.

People who feel goals tend to feel lighter and are very relaxed.

Your mind cannot tell the difference

As I said before, the mind cannot tell the difference between something that is vividly imagined and that which is real. That means that practice at mental picturing or creating movies in your head of the successful completion of your gymnastics skills and routines will benefit all the hard work you are doing in the gym.

Practice making mental movies of yourself competing and achieving your goals with confidence!

**Reprinted by permission of
Inside Gymnastics magazine.**

Mental Mock Meet

A "mock meet" is a practice meet many times with judges in attendance that takes place at your gym club so you can practice exactly like you would at a competition.

In a normal mock meet you will wear your competition leotard, do your hair, and prepare just like you would in competition. The idea is to get some realistic feedback to help you perform better during a real competition.

Movies in your head

A mental mock meet is where you sit in a comfortable chair, take several deep breaths in through your nose holding each one for 5 to10 seconds and then breathe out until your stomach starts to suck inward.

Once you are relaxed, it is time to turn on the movie projector in your mind and do a mental mock meet, literally practice exactly what you want to do when you are at the competition for real.

As I have said before, there is a saying that is popular in gymnastics circles and it goes like this, "Practice makes permanent, only perfect practice makes perfect."

Just one problem with this thinking; if you could always practice perfectly there would be no need of a coach and hardly any need to go to practice. Your life would be just like the movies or some popular TV show on the subject.

The reality is we all make mistakes, so the focus should be to do your best on each attempt. Do the absolute best you can each and every time you perform the skill physically and mentally.

Perfect mental practice?

Just as you may make some mistakes in the real world, it may take you some time to get your mental practice in order. (Please see the section on Visualization for specific guidelines.)

Your gymnastics competition script

The purpose of this section is to give you a script, which you can follow and mentally review to prepare you for your best meet ever. You can run this mental mock meet any time you want and if you make a mistake, you can simply rewind and do it over again until you get it just right.

Competition Script

The scene opens as you arrive at the gymnastics competition 30-minutes before open warm-ups will start for your competitive group.

You have your gym bag with everything you need for the meet and your hair and light make up is perfect.

The first thing you do is go to the registration table, show your athlete membership card and be prepared to sign in. You may receive your competitor number but don't worry because your coach will already have it in their coaches packet. Many times your competitor number will be written on the back of a card that will be used by your coach to hand into the head judge. In some team competitions, the cards will be put in order by the coach designating the order in which you will compete. In some instances, you will be given a number that you may have to pin to the back of your leotard.

Now, that you are checked in, you wave good bye to your parents and go and locate your coach and the rest of your teammates.

You find your coach and your teammates in the open warm-up area already starting to stretch out.

You place your gym bag in a secure area away from the warm-up area to keep the area obstacle free.

At this point, you will want to insert the team warm-up strategy designed by your coaches. Some teams start by running around the floor, and then adding their teams choreographed "line drills" which consist of various leaps, jumps, skips, and of other moves needed to get the blood flowing.

After a quick cardio session, you follow the guidelines of your coach to stretch and warm-up properly. Remember, this is open warm-up, not timed warm-ups so no tumbling or gymnastics moves other than stretching.

Seeing that the uneven bars are open for bar sets your coach leads you over to take a turn.

Your grips and wrist wraps are readily available in your gym bag and you slip them on quickly as you go to bars.

As each of your teammates gets their bar sets you help with moving the springboard, landing mats, and tightening the cables.

When its your turn to check settings, you do a glide kip cast to get a feel for the low bar, then you climb up on the low bar, jump to the high bar and do a series of taps swings not only to get a feel for the high bar but to make sure your setting is correct.

Even if the coach, writes down your bar settings, make sure you memorize them also. You never know when a clipboard could go missing or another coach, not normally your bar coach, may have to set your bars during competition.

Remember, it is your body that will suffer the consequence of the wrong bar setting.

Moments later the announcement is made that timed warm-ups will soon start. The competition order will be different for each team, but you will normally start warm-up on the event you compete first/last(?).

The actual order you compete in will be listed on a sheet, which your coach will have. You will rotate in Olympic order, Vault, Bars, Beam and Floor Exercise. On bars and beam, you may have a timer who will call out your number when it is time for you to take your turn warming up.

You have already planned out a warm-up strategy with your coach so you know which skills to focus on during timed warm-ups.

Even so, you are paying close attention to your coach's cues during warm-up and remembering to always finish your warm-up time with a dismount even if you have already performed one.

Of course, on vault, you focus on completing as many vaults as possible during the time allotted.

Remember to check your board setting for vault and to always start from the same point on the runway for each vault.

There will be a tape measure secured to the floor along the edge of the vault runway. You can use this to determine your starting point for your run and where your board should be set in front of the vault table.

Timed warm-ups are now over and an announcement is made requesting all teams to line up for march-in.

If you were wearing a practice leotard during warm-ups, sometimes a good idea in hot, humid weather, you now need to quickly change in to our competition leotard and make your sure your hair and makeup is done right.

If you get the chance, and especially if you feel the need, use the bathroom now so there will be no need to leave the competition floor during the meet.

How have you done so far?

Have you been able to easily see each of these elements of the competition in your minds' eye?

Remember while you are doing this mental rehearsal that you can change anything by simply rewinding in your mind as many times as you need until you get it just right.

Another way to make this mental rehearsal more realistic is to five-sense it. That means to add to your imagery everything you might hear while competing like the floor music, the sound of the springboard on vault, or the crowd cheering a particularly good routine.

Of course, you will always imagine the crowd roaring their approval for your routine as well.

Now do the same thing with all your other senses. What do you feel when you are competing? What do you smell? What do you see? What do you taste?

Add all of this sensory feedback to your visualization.

Line up and march-in

You will now line up by teams to march-in and present to the audience. If you coach has not already determined an order, the most logical might be to line up from smallest to tallest so everyone in the audience can see all team members.

You will also want to have developed some form of salute or presentation pose when your team name is called out.

Once all the teams have been presented, the judges and the meet director will be announced, then you will face the flag and the National anthem will be played.

The announcer will then request each team to march to their first competitive event.

When you first get to the event, you will present yourself to the judges at that event. Say hello with a big, confident smile, and listen to any instructions the judges may give you.

On each event you will get a thirty second warm-up. Typically on floor and vault the first half of the competition team will do one or two vaults or one or two tumbling passes then begin competition. When the first half of the team has finished competing, the second half of the team will get their thirty second warm-up.

On bars and beam, the first two competitors will warm-up, then when the first gymnast is finished competing the third gymnast in that rotation will warm-up, the fourth gymnast will begin warming-up before the second gymnast starts to compete and so on through the end of the rotation.

The time has come, it's your turn for the thirty second touch warm-up. Focusing on the strategy you planned with your coach, you approach the apparatus and confidently move through your most important skills.

While the gymnast ahead of you is performing her routine you are mentally doing your routine and performing it flawlessly.

The judges call your number and you step up in front of them and give them a big salute along with a confident smile.

The judges signal you to begin your routine.

There really is nothing to think about now. You have focused at workout and worked hard and you have practiced the routine at least a million times in your mind. The only thing to do now is put your body on autopilot and perform the routine to the best of your ability.

You stick the landing on your dismount and turn to the judges and give them a big smile and a salute.

Your teammates and coach are waiting for you as you run back over to the on deck area ready to give you hugs and congratulations.

Typically, bars and vault will finish a few minutes ahead of beam and bars. Make sure you have all your equipment in your gym bag and that you are prepared to compete on the next event.

When the first rotation is over you will line up with your team and march to the next event and start the process of presenting to the judges, warming up, and then competing all over again.

When the last performer has finished her routine, the announcer will ask you to line up and march over to the awards area.

You take great delight in accepting awards for your performance as well as the performance of your teammates and the other competitors.

Tonight you get to bask in the glory of this competition.

Tomorrow you will ask your coach for feedback about what you can do to improve your routines in the next meet.

The End

So, now you have a good idea what will happen at each gymnastics competition. Of course, there will be differences between compulsory and optional competitions and between the different levels of competition.

Practice, practice, practice

Studies have found that the mind cannot tell the difference between an actual event and an event that is vividly imagined. That means that every time you mentally rehearse your routines for competition you are definitely helping yourself to improve. The beauty is you can practice mentally anywhere and at any time – unless you driving a car or operating heavy machinery.

(See the appendix for the document "Competition Visualization Script: Quick Notes".)

Gymnastics: Your Best Meet Ever!

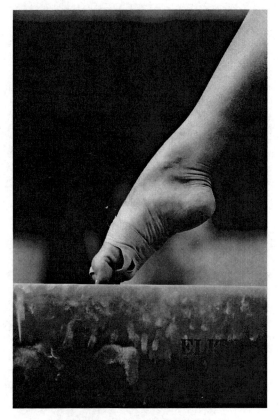

Reprinted by permission
Inside Gymnastics magazine.

Rita Brown

Reprinted by permission Inside Gymnastics magazine.

Competition – the real thing

Execution

The single largest area for potential loss in your score is in execution which can make up half or more of the total points possible in a given routine.

Execution or "form" as it is more commonly called in the gym is one of the most important factors in how well a routine scores.

For example, if one gymnast completed a beam routine and did not fall off, yet scored lower than someone who did fall and had a major wobble, wouldn't you start to wonder if the judges got it right?

If the first gymnast did her routine with poor form (bent knees, toes not pointed) throughout, even though she did not fall off, she could easily score much less than the gymnast who executes her routine with good form, grace, and amplitude - even with a fall.

Amplitude and extension

In addition to form or execution, amplitude and extension are very important.

Amplitude refers to the amount of power you show throughout your routine. An example of amplitude is the height you get while doing a split leap or blocking off the vault table.

Staying up on your toes on the beam is a good example of keeping the body fully extended.

Tenths of points will be taken here and there for a lack of amplitude or extension during the performance of your routine.

Presenting to the judge

After showing your competition number to the judge, you need to address the judges (a salute or presentation pose) before and after a gymnastics routine.

Practice saluting or presenting in front of a mirror or maybe in front of one of your parents. The idea is to look the judge in the eye with a calm, confident (not arrogant) expression, with a smile on your face that says you are there to show the judge the best you can do in this routine.

You must never act surprised when you make a skill in competition, it signals a possible lack of preparation which could cause the judges to scrutinize the routine closer. Simply smile!

Personal presentation

Make sure your hair is neatly combed and tied back out of your face. Your leotard should be clean and neat, and all gymnastics accessories (shoes, grips, etc.) must be clean and in good working order.

Make-up may sometimes be appropriate, if you happen to have very light skin, but never over do it. The idea is to emphasize your features only.

Recovering from a break or fall

Falls and major breaks are a fact of life in gymnastics competition from the lowest levels to Olympic level, so you will need to mentally rehearse what to do after a fall from a piece of equipment or a major break in your routine.

Many gymnasts will rush to get back on the equipment without thinking about where she left off in the routine – but not you! You will stop and take two or three deep breaths and mentally prepare for the rest of the routine.

Did you actually complete your last skill? Where should you begin the routine again? This is important to focus on because an element that is repeated will be a deduction.

Usually, a fall from a piece of equipment will result in a five tenths (half of one point) deduction.

Judging becomes difficult for the spectator and gymnast to understand when a fall occurs and the element preceding the fall is not completed. In this case, the value of the element (gymnastics skill) plus the deduction for the fall are taken, which results in a much lower score.

For example: If a routine on the balance beam has a handstand straddle down in it, and the gymnast falls off of the beam without completing the straddle down she loses the value of the handstand straddle down (for this example, we will say it is worth six tenths of a point) plus the deduction for the fall (five tenths of a point), for a total deduction of one and one tenth points. With this deduction the gymnast can receive a maximum score of an 8.90 out of a possible 10.00 for her routine, if she has no other falls or form breaks.

Note: Judges may give partial credit for an element depending on how much of it was completed before the fall.

Re-mounting the apparatus

On bars, the gymnast will have thirty seconds to chalk up and begin her routine again.

On balance beam the gymnast will have ten seconds to remount and continue. This time should be taken to mentally prepare for the rest of the routine.

Injury?

If your fall is a bad one, it is important to ascertain whether you are injured before returning to the routine. Take a moment and catch your breath, let your coach make sure you are okay before finishing the routine.

Time limits

Beam and floor exercise are the only events that have a time limit.

At the compulsory level, routine times may be different according to the level of competition.

For instance, a level five beam routine has a time limit of one minute and five seconds. After fifty five seconds a timer will call "warning" and you would now you have ten seconds to dismount without receiving a penalty deduction. The stop watch stops when your feet hit the mat.

It used to be that the judge would stop evaluating your routine once time was called. You automatically lost points for all uncompleted skills. Today, you can finish the routine and only have a few tenths deducted from your score for running over, rather than being forced to omit elements from your routine which can add up to whole points in deductions.

Falls stop timing

If a fall occurs during the routine, the timer will stop the clock until you have remounted the apparatus and restarted the routine.

Stick your landing

When you dismount from a piece of equipment, your landing is the last thing the judge will see so it is important that you "stick" (land in one spot without moving) your landing.

Each step you take on a landing can cost one tenth of a point, while landing on your seat can cost as much as five tenths of a point.

Stick your landings!

Specific deductions

There are deductions written for each element in a routine, such as how high a cast must be on the bars, or how far from the vault table you must land.

Each of these are specific to the level of competition and in fact the numbers and types of deductions for all the compulsory skills at each level fill a very large book (USAG Compulsories).

There are so many factors that go into the judging and scoring of a routine that it would take a separate book to describe all the errors and deductions.

In fact, there is such a book and a CD available for purchase for the compulsory routines that shows all the routines and possible deductions for each routine. (See the USA Gymnastics online store or address in the Resource section for more information)

Attitude / General Impression

There are specific points that may be deducted from your routine for a poor attitude or an overall sloppy impression.

It is important to remember when you have had a bad routine to smile and put forth the attitude "that is not like me, I can do better than that." If instead you pout or start to cry, you will make a very bad impression on the judges and be marked down for it.

Crying and feeling sorry for yourself is not an appropriate response to this situation or to most learning situations in the gym or in normal life.

Improving scores

Gymnastics is a sport of body lines, explosive power, and flexibility.

Body lines

Have you ever noticed that as the difficulty level increases the number of body lines decreases? The body generally has a minimum of three or four lines when doing a skill in the tuck position, two lines in the pike position and one line in the layout position.

So, a double back somersault in the tuck position is great, a double back in the pike position is amazing, but a double back in the layout position is awesome!

Once you have learned to do a skill using the least number of lines, practically the only way to add difficulty to it is to add a twist.

While you may not being doing double layouts with a twist yet, the basic concept is the same for all gymnasts on all the gymnastics apparatus: point your toes, keep your knees tight, suck in your stomach and tuck your seat under to maintain the best body lines possible (of course, appropriate to the skill being performed).

Strength

Again, it cannot be repeated too many times, strength is the ultimate technique you need to master. Have you ever watched an Olympic gymnastics event and seen a gymnast pull back a handstand on the uneven bars and save a skill when it seemed certain the gymnast would fall? A big part of that save was strength.

Or, have you ever seen a gymnast finish a tumbling skill on balance beam and it seemed certain she was going to fall, yet through the strength in her feet and toes she seemed to levitate back onto the beam? Strength!

When you think you are strong enough, think again. Strength is one of the key basics or foundation elements that needs constant attention if you want to be successful in competition.

Flexibility

Having great strength will be of little use to you unless you are flexible. You need to be as strong as possible through the greatest range of motion possible.

Attitude

The best thing you can wear to a gymnastics competition is a confident smile. Looking fidgety, jittery, and nervous telegraphs to the judges that you don't feel prepared for the competition.

Keep in mind that every winner was once a beginner.

You are allowed to make mistakes; it is the only way you will learn. The key is to always maintain the attitude of "I'll do my best" and the best way to demonstrate that attitude is to stand up straight, put your shoulders back, and look the head judge in the eyes with a confident smile on your face.

Scores

Of course, you always want the best score you are capable of, but that may not be the goal in every meet. To learn how to compete effectively you have to be willing to follow your coach's directions.

Winning is not always the goal, especially at the start of a season. Your coach may have you focus on getting a qualifying score only – the medals can wait for the championship meets. If the coach does that early in the season, the remaining meets before championships can be used to refine elements of the routines without the need to worry about qualifying.

In another meet, the coach may focus on introducing new skills to your routines or ramping up the power on the skills you already perform. You don't want to wait until the championship meet to finally go full power and pull out all the stops and maybe have to take a step on the dismount because you aren't used to the extra power.

That means in some meets you may have some falls or extra steps in landings as you learn to control the power of the skill, but since you are practicing these techniques in the lead up meets, you will likely have much better control than most gymnasts at the championship meet.

The meaning of a score

Always remember that a score is only the evaluation of one routine in your career as a gymnast. Because you get a 9.50 on one apparatus does not mean you will get a similar score on the next event or the same score in the next meet on the same apparatus.

The same is true if you get a much lower score.

The wisdom to make good choices in competition comes from experience.

Experience comes from making choices and decisions in previous competitions that have had both good and bad results and whether you use that information to your benefit or as a reason to sulk.

When you know better, you can do better. Apply all your experiences in competition toward making yourself a better competitor.

You can make an excuse or you can make an effort

The bars are too rough!

The beam is crooked!

The springboard is dead!

There are holes in the floor!

The bottom line is that the competition conditions are exactly the same for every gymnast at the meet.

Will complaining or getting upset make any difference?

Obviously, if you notice some condition that will affect your safety or the safety of other gymnasts you need to speak up - that is tell your coach so he/she can check it out and notify the meet director , if necessary.

Remember, you are most likely to do in the meet what you do in practice, so prepare in workout for what may happen in the meet.

For instance, if you like the bars rough with chalk, every now and then sand them down until they are smooth, then practice skills sequences to get a feel for what it may be like in a meet when the gymnast up before you decides to sand the bars smooth.

Speak up

Is the beam too high? Are there enough springs in the springboard? Is the music on floor loud enough?

Complaining after the fact will not help you get a better score. If you have any concerns, always present them to your coach in a timely fashion, but be prepared because sometimes a situation will be common to every gymnast in the meet and you can either make an excuse or you can make an effort to overcome the distraction /setback/ less than ideal condition.

Solutions for common mistakes / mishaps

Torn grips

Gymnastics grips get a lot of wear and tear throughout the season, so what happens if the grips you are comfortable with fall apart at the end of the year championships?

The answer is you will get your back-up pair of rips out of your gym bag and continue with the meet with no problem at all. The point is to always have two pairs of rips that you have broken in and are comfortable wearing so if one pair falls apart you have a back up ready to go.

Rips

A rip of the skin on the palm of the hands or on the wrists is a common occurrence in this sport. Likely you will have had a rip during normal workouts and your coach will ask you to clean it up, tape it, and continue workouts. This is not cruel and unusual punishment, this is training for the possibility of having a rip during a championship meet. (See the article "Caring for your rips" in the appendix)

Lucky stuffed animal

Oh no, you forgot your favorite (lucky) stuffed animal! Fortunately, since all your luck or preparation, focus, and attitude are present within you, you will still be able to compete with confidence and competence and you can tell Teddy all about when your bring back home your awards.

Different floor music

The key to your success in gymnastics competition is your ability to adapt to each situation. Listen to the music play during warm ups and mentally do a walkthrough of the routine. When other gymnasts compete before you in the lineup, mentally picture yourself going through all of the elements. The music may seem strange but the timing should be virtually the same with the compulsory music.

Optional floor music

Your coach should have a master copy of every team member's music on his iPhone or other digital device, but it won't hurt for you to bring a backup copy of your floor music in your gym bag just in case.

Equipment problems

The beam is crooked. The bars are too rough. The springboard is too hard. I can't get any punch out of the floor!

You can make an excuse, or you can make an effort to do your best with what you've got, and by the way, what every other gymnast in the meet has got to deal with.

Again, one of the attributes of a champion is her ability to adapt and deal with the situation in a positive and confident manner. It doesn't mean the problem does not exist, it simply means the problem is there, so how can you most effectively deal with it?

Talk to your coach about the problem and see if he or the meet director can rectify the situation.

If the problem is not a safety issue and it still persists and you and everyone else must compete and deal with it, you can shine above the rest by maintaining a positive attitude and working through it while others complain and make excuses for poor performance.

Judges make you wait

There will be times when the judges must confer over a score and you will have to wait a bit longer before you can compete. Use that time to take five deep breaths to calm and center yourself. Review a mental movie of the successful completion of your routine. When the judges signal they are ready, you will be too, to do the best routine possible.

Fall or major wobble

If you have a fall or a major wobble during a routine, you must continue regardless. You can pout and be upset and let that affect your performance or like mental picturing techniques you can put it behind you and finish the routine as if you never had a fall. Always do your best!

Note: If you do have a hard fall off the gymnastics apparatus, take a moment to assess any potential injury. I have seen gymnasts hit the floor hard and jump right back on the equipment without taking a moment to collect their thoughts or even to see if they are injured.

Take a moment to collect your thoughts, determine where you should start the routine from again, check your equipment, chalk up again, if you have to, and above all make sure you are fit to safely complete the routine.

Carrying forward mistakes

You finish a routine that has had a major mistake or fall. Salute the judges and make sure you give them a big smile.

Okay, you have permission to feel bad for about ten seconds, then you need to shake it off and focus on your next competition rotation. You can focus on what you need to do better next time after the meet is over.

Right now, you get a new beginning at a different event; it is time to leave the last event behind. Making a mistake on one event does not mean you will make a mistake on any other event.

I have to pee!

Obviously, the easy answer is to use the restroom just before you line up for competition. You certainly do not want to miss your turn by not being on the competition floor when it is your turn to compete.

Note: Make sure your coach knows where you are if you must leave the competition area. It is always a good idea to go with another gymnast instead of by yourself.

Anxiety may be another cause of your need to use the bathroom. Negative self-talk, nervousness, and other worries about competing may contribute to this condition.

Stop your negative train of thought and focus on the mental movie you have created for this event. As you preview the movie in your mind of how well your routine is going to be performed, take ten deep breaths in through the nose, hold for a few seconds, the exhale completely until your bellybutton almost touches your back bone.

Parents expect too much from you

It takes a number of years of quality competition for you to develop the poise and grace to continuously take top honors in a gymnastics competition.

With regard to expectations, the questions to ask yourself are:

Did I do a better floor routine this time than last?

Did I finally stick my vault?

Did I stay on the beam?

The key is to recognize when you are working up to your potential and any improvement no matter how incremental is a cause for celebration.

Sometimes just making an improvement in confidence is a critical improvement.

In gymnastics, winning occurs at many different levels. Achievement of a single skill for the first time without help from the coach is a significant form of winning.

If you do a routine and finish all your skills for the first time, making it through without falling off is a winning routine regardless of what score you receives.

Remember always that a score given to you in a gymnastics competition is an evaluation of one single performance, not an evaluation of you.

Other ways you can win at a meet include:

- sticking landings,

- improving scores,

- qualifying to higher level meets,

- learning to control the jitters,

- enjoying the competition,

- feeling part of the team,

- supporting fellow teammates,

- or just getting a pat on the back from the coach.

These are all important ways in which you win, which your parents and the public at large may not recognize but you can take pride in their accomplishment.

FOCUS: Follow One Coach Until Successful

One very important key to successful competition is to follow your coach's instructions. Everyone from former gymnasts, parents and relatives, and other gymnasts on your team may be free in giving you advice. They are all well meaning and likely have your best interests at heart, but the only advice you should follow is the advice your coach gives you in practice and at competition.

The bottom line is you can only follow one set of directions. The only result of trying to follow too many sets of directions is confusion and a lack of concentration that can lead to worry and becoming nervous. *Follow One Course Until Successful* – the one your coach sets for you.

Why can't I use my cell phone?

You can use your cell phone to store your favorite motivational music or download a video of you doing your best routines, but while you are at the meet your focus should be on competition, not texting your friends or family.

Note: Most definitely make sure the ringer on your phone is turned off. The last thing you want to do is cause a distraction for yourself or others.

The best time to use your cell phone is after the meet is over and you are on the way home when you can text all your friends about how well you did at the competition.

Sportsmanship

The crowd roars with approval as you strike the finishing pose of a flawlessly performed routine. Screaming and hugging are the order of the day as everyone celebrates the performance.

The next and final gymnast to perform, the only one with a chance of beating your score to win the championships passes by you on her way to perform. One of your younger team members calls out to her, "Good luck, you're going to need it!"

While watching the performance standing near the bleachers you hear parents say, "I hope she falls on her first tumbling pass so our team wins."

Wow! What's going on here? Is this good sportsmanship?

I wouldn't want any team I coached to ever win by default or to publicly display such behavior. The point of entering a competition is to test yourself against another competitor of equal or even superior abilities. When you win, you really have some bragging rights. Defeating a weaker athlete does nothing to test your preparation and training skills or demonstrate your competence.

It is always disturbing to hear nice people wishing negative consequences on worthy rivals.

Some may attempt to justify unsportsmanlike conduct as strategy, and inappropriate comments as "letting off steam," but think how any young gymnast would feel hearing a comment of that nature directed toward her.

What does it mean to win?

W.I.N?

W.I.N? stands for What's Important Now?

The answer is adopting the mission statement "win generously, lose graciously, and develop character constantly." That is what is important now and at every competition.

Winning generously simply means that you coach your team to always do its best in any competition, respect and learn from your competitors, and appreciate every performance remembering that every athlete is doing the best she can at the moment – in other words, every winner was once a beginner.

Losing graciously means congratulating your opponent for providing a competition that gave you an insight into areas that need improvement.

A loss to an impressive opponent can still be chalked up in the win category if you achieved a personal best or simply demonstrated a higher level of performance.

Developing character constantly is demonstrated by not giving up, by overcoming obstacles, and keeping a good attitude whether your team wins or loses.

The storyline of the classic movie Rocky is appropriate to this topic. A down and out boxer in Philadelphia is offered a chance in the ring to box the world champion Apollo Creed.

Rita Brown

Didn't Rocky win just by standing toe to toe with Apollo Creed even though he lost the fight?

Although Apollo Creed won the fight, didn't he lose in his own estimation and in the eyes of the public and the boxing community by not being able to convincingly and overwhelmingly win over Rocky?

Have you and your team had some "Rocky" moments?

While the definition of winning is, in part, determined by the goals of the competitive system, the desires of the athlete and coach, and the scoring / judging system used, it is mostly a byproduct of attitude and a belief in the ability to constantly improve.

No single competition or performance ever defines a gymnast or a team. Any performance is simply that, a onetime presentation of skill, not an albatross of shame to carry with you to the next competition.

Sportsmanship is something all children learn and model by watching the significant adults in their lives; Mom and Dad, relatives, teachers, and coaches to name a few.

As a gymnast, you must model the behaviors you expect from your teammates.

Behavior is always a choice for which you must take responsibility. Be supportive to other teammates, acknowledge disappointments (yours and others), but do not tolerate unacceptable behavior.

You might want to help educate your parents on the rules of a gymnastics competition and what to expect from the scoring system.

Summary

Go into any gym and look at the wealth of trophies lining the walls. The very icons of achievement fought so hard for in one brief moment of time are literally put on a shelf and forgotten until they are covered with cobwebs and dust.

Rita Brown

Memories, character, and the shared
experience are all that count in the end.

Do You Have What It Takes?

15 minutes of fame

It has been said that everybody gets at least 15 minutes of fame within her lifetime.

When you add up all the time that a female gymnast actually performs in a gymnastics competition that time frame seems just about right.

If you figure that the floor exercise and beam routines are one minute thirty seconds each, the bar routines takes about one minute, and two vaults at thirty seconds each that comes out to about 5 minutes of actual competition.

If you count the approximately 10 minutes of warm up time per meet for a total of fifteen minutes of potential fame in a local gymnastics invitational.

Wow, the best fifteen minutes of your life!

But, are you willing to put in the hundreds of hours it will take to get to that level?

My purpose in bringing this to your attention is to have you focus on just what kind of attention do you want to get out of your involvement with this sport.

Fame and success are defined not only by the individual, but the club and the community in which you live.

Sometimes just making your routines and making your parents proud is all the fame you need.

Helping the team to win a trophy by hitting your beam routine feels great, especially when your teammates surround you with hugs.

Winning state championships on one event or the all around and getting your name in the local newspaper is superb.

But, each of these levels of fame is attained based on the effort and commitment you put in to your workouts.

The key to getting your fifteen minutes of fame is personal responsibility.

Gymnastics: Your Best Meet Ever!

What other gymnasts do during workout is their problem, their fault, and their responsibility, not an excuse for you to have similar behavior.

You need to accept the consequences and the credit for your behavior during workouts.

Remember that behavior is made up of attitude, ability to follow directions, focus and follow through with assigned drills and techniques, as well as how you relate to teammates and coaches.

Obviously, by the very fact that you made it this far in the book shows that you are an individual that finishes what she starts.

If you combine your ability to commit to a goal and add an abundance of desire, I have no doubt that you will shortly have your best meet ever!

Congratulations!

Appendix

**Reprinted by permission of
Inside Gymnastics magazine.**

Questions to focus your goals

- I started gymnastics because...

- I wanted to be on the team and compete because...

- This is what my coach looks like:

- My coach's favorite sayings are...

- My best friends on the team this year are...

- The night before a meet I am ...

- The thing I like most about competition at Level 4 is...

- The thing I would most like to change about competition at Level 4 is...

- My favorite event is _____ and the reason why is...

- The event I need to improve most is _____ and the reason why is...

Rita Brown

- I am really good at...

- The thing I liked best in my goody bag this season was...

- Just before competing for the very first time I felt like...

- The thing I remember most about this season is...

- When my friends at school ask about gymnastics, I tell them...

- My favorite thing to eat before a meet is...

- My favorite event is the...

- My current goal in gymnastics is to...

- The most important thing I learned from my coach is...

- The most important thing I would tell a new level 4 gymnast is...

- My top ten most favorite things about gymnastics are...

- Describe the perfect gym meet.

Gymnastics: Your Best Meet Ever!

- My favorite thing to do after a meet is…

- Use 10 or more single word adjectives to describe yourself as a competitive gymnast.

- List your positive traits (behaviors, qualities, characteristics) as a competitive gymnast.

- Make a list of things you would like to improve about yourself as a gymnast.

- Describe the perfect gymnastics meet.

- Who is the first person you want to call and tell all about the meet when it is over?

- What do you say to yourself after a particularly good meet?

- What do you say to yourself after a particularly bad meet?

(Can you improve your self-talk so everything you said internally helps you grow and get better?)

Homework

Homework is an annoying fact of life, however, it is also an important discipline to learn that will help you succeed later in life. Homework is like conditioning after workout. You might not like it, but you know it is necessary.

Homework conditions your mind to be stronger and at the same time flexible and open to new ideas which will help you with your school work and with understanding new and different techniques in the gym.

Here are some suggestions that will help make homework easier and more fun to do.

Suggestion #1: Do your homework when you first get home from school. That means right away, not after you watch some television, or talk to friends on the phone for an hour. Your mind will still be in the schoolwork mode. It will be much easier to follow through and get the homework done than it will be to get back in the mood after you have started something else.

Suggestion #2: Keep all distractions to a minimum. Doing homework with the television on or your IPOD blasting your favorite tune divides your attention. Keep focused on the work at hand and it will be finished much sooner.

Suggestion #3: Pick a place where you will have access to all the materials you need to complete the assignment. Using the same place every day will also condition your brain to get right to work once you are settled in.

Suggestion #4: Keep a small pad or section of your notebook for accurately writing down exactly what your homework assignments are for each day. Check the pad before you leave school to be sure you have all the books or materials you need to complete your assignments. Many teachers now post homework assignments along with resources on a web site. Check with each of your teachers for the appropriate web address.

Suggestion #5: Use different techniques to review the important parts of your assignments or potential test questions. A couple of ideas are:

* Highlight the material with different color pens depending on the type of information. (I.E. historical dates in blue, famous names in yellow, etc.)

* Read important information aloud into a tape recorder while playing relaxing music in the background. Listen to the tape at night while you sleep.

* On many computers you can connect a microphone to make a digital file of your important class notes that you can download to an IPOD or MP3 player to listen to and review materials for tests on the way to school or during study periods.

* Use index cards. Write specific bits of information you need to know on one side of the card, and a question pertaining to the information on the other side. You now have a series of flash cards that you can shuffle randomly to quiz yourself on information that may come up on a test.

Gymnastics: Your Best Meet Ever!

Each of these ideas will help you to get your homework done a little bit easier and quicker while remembering more of the information. Remember to pay extra close attention during class and ask as many questions as you need to understand the information from your teacher. The better you pay attention in class the more you will understand and the easier the homework assignments will be.

Don't wait to talk to your teacher, parents, or coach if you are having difficulty with homework or a subject in school. If necessary, your coach may be able to set up workout programs that will enable you to maintain your present physical condition while you get caught up on your school work.

Be warned that this is only a short-term measure. Higher level optional skills need to be practiced on a regular basis for safety and consistency, but if push comes to shove; education always comes first, which could result in a change of your competitive status.

Talk to your teacher at school and let her know that you are a competitive athlete and that you workout a few nights a week. The teacher may be able to suggest some ideas for better study habits, or she may revise your homework schedule. Do not expect to get out of homework because you are a competitive athlete.

Ask your teacher if she can set aside some time to help you before or after school with any subjects you may have a problem with. Many schools offer afterschool study groups to help with class and homework problems.

Around the country a number of "Homework Hotlines" are set up where you can call a teacher who will give you ideas on how to solve your homework problems. Contact your school for the phone numbers in your area. In addition, there are several online sites for help with homework issues.

Do You Have The Time?

How much time do you allow to get your homework done? Many gymnasts, by the very nature of the sport, are quite organized. They have learned to get a lot done in the little time available to them. Make sure that you are providing yourself adequate time to get your work done.

A simple chart listing your daily activities should give you an idea of whether you are being more "active" than "productive." You may need to drop some of your other activities to enable yourself to effectively finish your schoolwork and still have time to workout at the gym.

Your education is more important than anything else - even gymnastics! Even your coaches must continue to study and keep informed of new developments in the sport.

Communicate with your coach, your parents, and your teachers when you are having a problem with your school work. Each will help you to learn how to solve your problems so you can get back in the gym and reach your gymnastic goals.

Rita Brown

Reprinted by permission
Of Inside Gymnastics magazine.

Take care of your hands

Rips are a common, though painful occurrence in the sport of gymnastics. Everyone gets them from the beginner to the elite level performer. For the novice gymnast, rips normally occur because the gymnast's grip on the bar is too tight because of fear or lack of familiarity with the skill. Advanced gymnasts usually rip because they allow an excess of callous to develop on their hands.

A rip is a separation of the upper layers of skin in the palm of the hand or around the wrists from the lower layers of blood rich tissue.

An excessively tight grip or callous buildup allows the skin to bunch up as you are swinging around the bar. The force of the swing pulls the upper layer of skin away from the lower layers causing a pocket to form which may become a blister or fill with blood. Whichever occurs, you can be sure that a rip is imminent.

Another form of a "rip" occurs around the gymnast's wrists where a hand guard or "grip" may continuously rub against the skin.

Usually, a combination of tennis sweatbands for the wrist, gym tape and/or pre-wrap can be used to cover the area and prevent a rip.

If a rip does occur on the wrist, get the first aid pads used for plantar warts that are usually oval in shape and have a hole in the center. Position the pad over the rip so the hole is directly over the injured area, then tape it in place and put sweat bands and grips on top.

Swing technique

For the novice gymnast, simple training in appropriate swing techniques and grip change will help alleviate several rips.

For the more advanced gymnast, a daily regimen of hand care must be put into effect to minimize rips and keep bar workout times more effective.

Before You Rip

1. After every workout wash your hands with soap and water, then rub hand lotion into the front and back of your hands and wrists.

2. Prevent excess callous from building up by rubbing the affected areas with a pumice stone.

   To find the areas of excess callous, soak the hands in water for about ten minutes and you will be able to notice areas on the palm that retain a whitish color while the rest of the skin stays pink.

   Use the pumice stone only as necessary. Excessive use will cause the hands to be constantly sore during workouts.

3. Rub hand lotion into your hands at night before going to sleep and, if necessary, when you get up in the morning. Always keep your hands moist.

When You First Rip

1. Remove the excess skin carefully. A sterilized pair of nail clippers (to prevent infection) should work nicely, then wash the injured area with soap and water.

   Don't put hand lotion on a fresh rip. Cover the rip with some "over-the-counter" antibiotic ointment rather than Vaseline so the injured area has a chance to breathe.

   Some pharmacies carry products called "Second Skin" or "NewSkin" that comes in patch or liquid form and may be placed directly over the rip although some products sting as much as iodine when placed on a fresh rip.

2. Before going to sleep at night, put some antibiotic ointment on the rip and cover your hand with a sock or glove (with finger holes cut out) to keep the ointment off the sheets and out of your eyes. This treatment should continue until the rip is covered with new skin.

After You Have Ripped

1. Once new skin has covered the rip, continue using hand lotion as described above. If the rip is allowed to dry up, the skin will crack and you will continue to rip in the same spot. Sometimes rubbing Chapstick over a drying rip can also prevent cracking.

2. If you must work out again after ripping, do not cover the rip with the sticky side of the tape. Instead lay a small piece of tape "sticky-side up" over the rip so it comes in contact with the sticky-side of the tape you are putting over the rip to protect the injured area.

On nights when you have particularly hard workouts on bars and your hands are hot and throbbing, it is a good idea to soak your hands in cool water or hold ice cubes in your hands (wrapped in a moist paper towel) until they melt. This will help the inflamed tissues to cool off.

Just before a competition, you can deaden the pain of a rip by keeping an ice pack on it, or soaking the hands in a slush bath of ice water for ten minutes. This will help keep your concentration on the routine instead of the pain of the rip. **Note**: Make sure your hands are back to room temperature before competing.

Discipline yourself to take care of your hands before and after every workout so that when your chance comes to make it big in the championship meet, you will be fully prepared for success.

Special Note: Wear protective latex gloves when working with an open wound.

Tape grips

Ask your coach to show you how to make a pair of tape grips that will give you an extra layer of protection and lessen the pain of the rip.

Gymnastics: Your Best Meet Ever!

Gym bag checklist

Before each competition make sure the following items are in your gym bag:

- ☐ Uneven bar grips (plus extra set), wrist wraps, gymnastics tape and hand lotion.

- ☐ A back up copy of your Optional (and/or compulsory) Floor music.

- ☐ Team competition leotard.

- ☐ Team warm-up suit.

- ☐ Hair care, make-up, and personal hygiene items.

- ☐ Any vital medical braces, supports, or bandages.

- ☐ Medical Release Form, necessary medicines, and emergency phone numbers.

- ☐ Cell phone for emergencies and money for meals on the road.

Additional items you may wish to have with you during away meets:

Gymnastics: Your Best Meet Ever!

☐ An extra leotard for warm ups (clean).

☐ Gymnastics slippers.

☐ Hand towel (when it's hot).

☐ Water in unbreakable container (mostly necessary during hot/humid weather).

☐ Small first aid kit for the care of rips, scrapes, etc. [1]

☐ Sneakers & Peds (gymnastics socks) or flip flops.

☐ Jump rope (to facilitate stretching exercises and cardiovascular work and warm up drills).

☐ Spiral bound pad and pen, leisure reading book or Kindle, cards, or video game.

☐ Fruit slices or crackers in re-sealable bag to snack on when the meet runs long.

---

[1] (Band-Aids, gauze pads, nail clippers, antibacterial spray, and soap)

Rita Brown

Travel checklist

- ☐ The exact time open warm-ups start and specifically when your coach wants you to be at the gym ready to compete.

- ☐ The exact address to the meet site – not the address to the gym of the team hosting the meet. Note: You may want to drive over to the meet site the night before to determine the best route in the morning, discover any traffic issues, and the best place to park.

- ☐ A GPS is great but even better is a current map with the route marked out. (Some online programs may have you twisting and turning all over the place!)

- ☐ The cell phone number for your coach in case you get lost.

Note: You may want to stay overnight in a hotel for meets that start at the crack of dawn.

Gymnastics: Your Best Meet Ever!

☐ Bring your own alarm clock or set your cell phone in case the wakeup call from the front desk is late or missing.

☐ Bring your own pillow for comfort in the hotel room and sleeping in the car.

☐ Put out everything you will need the night before so you are not searching madly the next morning for your leotard, hair ties, etc.

☐ Snacks and possibly some breakfast items in a cooler in case the hotel restaurant is crowded. It's probably best to eat at least two hours before warm-ups.

Competition Visualization Script – Quick Notes:

- Arrive at competition site.
- Check-in for competitor number.
- Find coach and teammates.
- Start open warm-up.
- Get bar settings, board settings on vault.
- Start timed warm-ups on each event.
- Help with setting equipment.
- Be prepared for your turn. Focus on the warm-up strategy developed with your coach.
- Line up, march in, national anthem.
- March to first event and present to judges.
- Focus on strategy for touch warm-up.
- Compete effectively and finish with confidence. Remember, salute and smile.
- Continue competing effectively on each event.
- After completing competition, line up and march to the awards area.
- Demonstrate your sportsmanship by acknowledging every gymnast's effort whether she is a teammate or not.
- Enjoy the moment!

Your goal sequence / focus
(Beginning of the season)

Develop physical strength and flexibility to the highest level you can based on guidelines provided by your coach.

Be able to perform each of the elements required on each event.

Be able to perform each of the elements required on each event in a sequence of three or four skills.

Successfully perform the front half of each routine.

Successfully perform the back half of each routine.

(At least one month prior to competition.)

Perform the whole routine.

Successfully perform the whole routine without any falls or major wobbles.

Successfully perform the whole routine with confidence and competence enough to score a minimum of an 8.00 or better on each event.

(Beginning of competitive season.)

Attend the first invitational meet of the season and make the qualifying score for state championships.

Refine my routines in each of the invitational meets so I am adding a minimum of a full point to my all around score each meet.

Focus on going full out on my routines so I can control each of the elements under full power and stick all my landings perfectly.

(All your hard work

peaks at championships.)

I am the State Champion in the all around competition. *(Yeah!)*

Note: Check with your coach for the appropriate timeline to achieve each of these goal elements.

Additional goal setting techniques

1. Write down all your goals on 3' x 5' cards and place them around you room so you will see them and focus on them often.

2. Create "Treasure Maps." A treasure map is a graphic representation of the goal you would like to achieve. You can cut pictures out of magazines, draw the skills, paste ribbons for first place on an event, put the part of the score sheet with your "goal" scores on to one piece of construction paper and create your own treasure map for what you would like to achieve.

3. Write your goal down in as much detail as possible creating an autobiography of your successful season.

4. Develop a "trigger". Pick some object or item that every time you see it will cause you to focus on your goal for a moment to give it a little more mental energy to speed the goal on its way to a successful conclusion.

Rita Brown

**Reprinted by permission of
Inside Gymnastics magazine.**

Specific Meet Goals

Name of Meet:

Date:

Location:

My focus in general warm-up is:

My focus in timed warm is:

Vault:

Bars:

Beam:

Floor:

My main goal in this meet is:

My goal is to score:

Vault:

Bars:

Beam:

Floor:

All Around:

Rita Brown

Is it okay to miss workout?

The short answer to that question is no. Remember, the main goal of this book is to show you how to have your best meet ever. To achieve that goal you need to make workout consistently, and not just make workout but be there on time for stretching and proper warm-up and also finish workout properly with conditioning and flexibility drills instead of leaving workout early.

Significant Life Events

There are times when missing a workout may be appropriate, but it should be the exception rather than the rule.

For instance, I don't believe you should miss what I call **"significant life events."** Life events could be attending the wedding of a family member, graduating from school, earning a special reward, a religious ceremony, or your birthday party.

The problem comes when **"significant life events"** become confused with **"non-**

critical social events." That's when you start missing workouts to attend birthday parties for each of your classmates, or you want to skip Friday workouts to go to football games, or you start coming late to workout because you also want to be on the school cheerleading squad.

None of these activities is bad or inappropriate except when they negate the commitment and responsibility you have accepted as a member of a competitive gymnastics team program.

Those are the key words: **commitment and responsibility**. When you join the team, you are making a commitment to the coach and the rest of the team to make every scheduled workout. By missing workouts you not only let down your teammates and your coach, you actively destroy the benefits of previous training and conditioning.

Effect of missed workouts

The reality is that missing one workout or more per week can cause:

♦ a loss of strength.

- a loss of flexibility.

- a loss of timing in the execution of skills.

- a loss of confidence in attempting skills without a spot.

- you to miss specific optional or compulsory technique training that may have been a "breakthrough" session leading to a higher level of skills.

- you to feel left out when unable to do new skills presented in your absence.

- other team members to be held back while a coach repeats training already presented.

- the coach to divide his/her attention between working remedial drills with you and other teammates training new skills.

- a bad habit to develop where you feel justified in missing workouts for increasingly inappropriate reasons.

Consistent workout participation is a necessary part of any sport and it is the coach's job to monitor and enforce this aspect of your commitment to the program.

Be a meaningful specific

Best-selling author and motivational speaker, Zig Ziglar, describes people as either **"wandering generalities"** or **"meaningful specifics."** Your gymnastics coach can best be described as a "meaningful specific" whose main focus or goal is the success of each and every team member including you.

When a problem arises with attendance it will be your coach's job to focus on your training needs and overall team interests first and your social interests second.

Commitment and responsibility are the key words you need to understand when you want to be a successful gymnast, however, re-evaluation of your priorities may be needed if you find there is no way you can keep to the schedule of workouts developed by the coaching staff. Perhaps scaling back your gymnastics goals or at the least taking a longer-term approach towards their achievement would be most appropriate.

In any event, if you find that you are going to miss a workout you should:

♦ Call the gym and notify the coaching staff in advance.

♦ Plan with the coach a time you can "make-up" the missed workout.

♦ Talk with your coach about a new strategy if other "priorities" in your life are going to interfere with previous "commitments."

Sticking to your commitments and responsibilities is important, but should something else grab your interest momentarily or for the long-term you owe it to the coaching staff and your fellow teammates to keep the lines of communication open and honest.

There is life before, during, and after the sport of gymnastics, however, while you are imitating superheroes and doing the near impossible in the gym, you need to make some sacrifices to achieve your goal of having your best meet ever!

Take time to smell the roses, but get to workout on time!

Basic gymnastics competition glossary

All Around – competition for a gymnast that includes vault, uneven bars, balance beam, and floor exercise.

All Around Score - A gymnast's total score from all events (I.E. vault, bars, beam, and floor).

Apparatus: A piece of equipment used in gymnastics training or competition.

Awards – if the organization running the meet is on the ball you may only have to wait five to ten minutes before the awards are handed out. It has been known to take significantly longer to get the awards ready. Once they are prepared it can take from fifteen minutes to half an hour to hand out the awards.

Balance beam: A sixteen-foot beam, 4-inches wide and approximately 4-feet above the floor, used for routines involving leaps, turns and tumbling moves in women's artistic gymnastics.

Chalk – a powder gymnast's use on their hands that helps reduce friction on the hands or may help to reduce moisture.

Competition – the gymnasts now actually compete and receive scores from the judges at each event. This may take an hour and a half to two hours to complete. Longer if it is an optional meet and one touch warm ups are necessary.

Competition order – a list of gymnast's numbers and the order they will compete on each event.

Compulsory Routines - A series of skills on each event that are put together with clearly marked timing, amplitude, and body position. The USAG develops a set of routines for Levels 2, 4, 5. All gymnasts compete using the routines developed by USA Gymnastics.

Difficulty: A rating that measures the difficulty of specific moves and is factored into the total score after judges have scored the execution of the moves.

Dismount: The final skill performed in a routine that must be stuck on landing that is to take no steps on completion and then salute to the judges.

Element: A single skill or dance movement that has been assigned a degree of difficulty and or value in a gymnastics routine.

Eligible - An active gymnast, current with USAG, club, and Booster fees, who, with coaches approval, may participate in all activities including meets and exhibitions.

Event Rotation – the competition order for each gymnastics apparatus.

Event specialist – a gymnast who focuses her competitive ability on one or two events and does not compete as an all around gymnast.

Execution: The form, style, amplitude, timing and technique used to complete the skills included in a routine in their appropriate sequence.

Flexibility: Flexibility is the range of motion through which a body part, such as the shoulders or legs, can move without feeling pain, while maintaining strength and stability of the joint.

Floor exercise: An event in men's and women's artistic gymnastics where a gymnast performs a series of exercises on an open 42' by 42' square of mats (with springs underneath) covered with carpet.

Gymnast number – a specific number assigned to each gymnast in a competition.

Invitational Meet - A meet, usually with a specific theme, hosted by any gymnastics club. These may or may not be qualifying meets for state championships, but scores may usually be used to move a gymnast from one level to the next.

Landing Mat: A four to eight-inch mat filled with foam and ethyfoam to soften the landing when a gymnast dismounts the apparatus.

March in – all the gymnasts line up and march in to the gym to be presented to the audience and judges. Usually the

National Anthem is played. This takes about ten to fifteen minutes.

Mobility Score – The score needed to move from one competitive level to the next. For example, a score of 31.00 all round may be needed to move from Level 4 to Level 5. The mobility score should not be confused with a "qualifying score" even if they are numerically the same.

Open warm up – Usually a half-hour long. This time is for general stretching and getting equipment settings specific to the gymnast.

Optional Routines - Routines developed and choreographed by the coaches for each gymnast to be used primarily[2] in levels 7, 8, 9, 10, & Elite. The routines will be individualized for each gymnast's strength, style, and difficulty.

---

[2] Some states also include a series of competitions for Novice Optional and Prep Optional gymnasts as an additional stage of preparation for the more difficult optional competitions.

Optionals: Routines created by the gymnast which portray their best skills and personality.

Qualifying Meet - A sanctioned meet where the scores are used to qualify for the State Meet. The number of meets actually scheduled will be determined by a gymnast's ability to successfully complete the appropriate level routines and receive the score necessary for state competition.

Qualifying Score – The all around score (total of vault, bars, beam, and floor) needed for entry into the state competition. Normally this score is determined by USA Gymnastics, but in some cases may be changed according to a particular state or region's needs.

Salute – a presentation pose adopted by a gymnast to signal her readiness to start a routine or to indicate the end of a routine.

Springboard / Vault Board: The device used to launch a gymnast into the air over a vault table. Usually has 3 to 6 springs mounted between two boards, the top board being covered with carpet.

Start / Finish pose – see Salute.

State Meet - In most cases, the season finale, where qualified gymnasts compete with other gymnasts throughout the state. Higher level gymnasts may go on to compete in regional or national level competitions.

Stick Landing – the finish of a routine where a gymnast lands without taking a step before saluting the judge or striking a finishing pose.

Timed warm-up - Every gymnast present warms up on each of the apparatus. This procedure can take from an hour to an hour and a half, sometimes more.

Uneven bars: An apparatus in women's artistic gymnastics with a top bar almost 10 feet above the floor and a lower bar 4 1/2' high, used for a continuous series of grip changes, releases, new grasps and other complex moves.

USAG - USA Gymnastics.

Vault: A solid apparatus similar to the pommel horse, but lacking handles, and used in men's and women's artistic gymnastics for a variety of handsprings from a running approach.

Rita Brown

**Reprinted by permission of
Inside Gymnastics magazine.**

Resources

Gymcert
www.gymcert.com
407-444-5669

GymCert is an authorized
education provider for
USA Gymnastics University

Inside Gymnastics magazine
http://www.insidegymnastics.com/
770.394.7160

PublishingSuccessOnline.com
(Is there a book inside you?)
www.PublishingSuccessOnline.com
Rik@PublishingSuccessOnline.com
407-529-8539

USA Gymnastics
http://usagym.org/pages/index.html
317-237-5050

Rita Brown

About the Author

 When I was thirteen years old, Gymnastics was something you did if you belonged to the YMCA. My family was middle class and my parents had six children for which I was number four. I wanted to attend the Y with my friends from school, but my mother said no. She had my five other sisters and brothers that needed taking care of and no time to drive me back and forth from the Desplain's YMCA which was located several towns over.

Finally, my continued desire to be a part of the sport landed me in the Deerfield Town District Saturday morning class program which gave me my early beginnings in the sport that over the years consumed my every waking and sleeping thought. In summary, gymnastics was now in my blood and I could not get enough of it.

I competed in High School and College. My high school coach, Sandy Oldham was probably the most inspirational coach I had. She motivated me to do better every day and taught me to be a good team player. College was awesome and at times I wished it would never end. Someone once told me that the best time your life is during college and they were right. Athletes are looked up to and admired by all. Students, Staff and community loved you and cheered for you. What a great feeling. I highly recommend it.

Title IX came about during the later days in my college life, thus no scholarship for me. Seeking out the best coaches landed me in Florida where I still live today.   I transferred the summer between sophomore and Junior years from The University of Wisconsin to the University of Florida so I could train with Sandy Phillips who was one of Vannie Edwards infamous College athletes who now was the head coach at U of F. A year and a half later I had a shoulder injury which caused my retirement from competition. So, I continued to teach during the summers back home as well as at a local gym club in Gainesville Fl. It was the summer before my senior year that I had the opportunity to buy out the local gym club from my professor, Joe Regna. I was only 21 years old and that was the beginning of the beginning. Over the years my passion grew stronger and stronger. My team kids were getting better and better. I grew as a coach and leader. Coaching is leadership. Successful coaching is winning through other people.

Over the years I have found that fundamentally all the lessons and principals of both a good sound business and good coaching all apply to the motivations and the aspiration to WIN. My success as a coach is directly related to my ability to assess, understand and apply the principals of strong leadership both in the gym and in all life situations.

Rita Brown

Ordering Information

To order additional copies of this book or to make bulk orders for groups go to:

www.gymcert .com

Rita Brown

193

Rita Brown

Gymnastics: Your Best Meet Ever!

Rita Brown

Competition Notes

Rita Brown

Gymnastics: Your Best Meet Ever!